7 TO 12:
A DETECTIVE STORY

Nadakkavu, Kozhikode, Kerala, 673011
www.insightpublica.com
e-mail: insightpublica@gmail.com

Title: **7 to 12 A Detective Story**
Author: **Anna Katharine Green**
First Insight Edition: August 2024
Copyright © Reserved
All rights reserved.
Printed and Published by
InsightinPublica Printers & Publishers Pvt. Ltd.
ISBN: 9789355177858

7 TO 12:
A DETECTIVE STORY

Anna Katharine Green

contents

7 TO 12
A DETECTIVE STORY

"Clarke?"

"Yes, sir."

"Another entrance through a second-story window. A detective wanted right off. Better hurry up there,—East Seventy-third Street."

"All right, sir."

Clarke turned to go; but the next moment I heard the Superintendent call him back.

"It is Mr. Winchester's, you know; the banker."

Clarke nodded and started again; but a suppressed exclamation from the Superintendent made him stop for the second time.

"I've changed my mind," said the latter, folding up the slip of paper he held in his hand. "You can see what Halley has for you to do; I'll attend to this." And giving me a look that was a summons, he whispered in my ear: "This notification was written by Mr. Winchester himself, and at the bottom I see hurriedly added, 'Keep it quiet; send your discreetest man.' That means something more than a common burglary."

I nodded, and the affair was put in my hands. As I was going out of the door, a fellow detective came hurriedly in.

"Nabbed them," cried he.

"Who?" asked more than one voice.

"The fellows who have been climbing into second-story windows, and helping themselves while the family is at dinner."

I stopped.

"Where did you catch them?" I asked.

"In Twenty-second Street."

"To-night?"

"Not two hours ago."

I looked at the Superintendent. He gave a curious lift of his brows, which I answered with a short smile. In another moment I was in the street.

My first ring at the bell of No.—East Seventy-third Street brought response in the shape of Mr. Winchester himself. Seeing me, his countenance fell, but in another instant brightened as I observed:

"You sent for a detective, sir;" and quietly showed him my badge.

"Yes," he murmured; "but I did not expect"—he paused. I was used to these pauses; I do not suppose I look exactly like the ordinary detective. "Your name?" he asked, ushering me into a small reception-room.

"Byrd," I replied. And taking as a compliment the look of satisfaction which crossed his face as he finished a hasty but keen scrutiny of my countenance and figure, I in turn subjected him to a respectful but earnest glance of interrogation.

"There has been a robbery here," I ventured.

He nodded, and a look of care replaced the affable expression which a moment before had so agreeably illumined his somewhat stern features.

"Twenty-five thousand dollars' worth," he whispered, shortly. "Mrs. Winchester's diamonds."

I started; not so much at the nature and value of the articles stolen, as at the indefinable air with which this announcement was made by the wealthy and potential broker and banker. If his all had been taken his eye could not have darkened with a deeper shadow; if that all had been lost through means which touched his personal pride and feelings, he could not have given a sharper edge to his tones, business-like as he endeavored to make them.

"A heavy loss," I remarked. "Will you give me the details of the affair as far as you know them?"

He shook his head and waved his hand with a slight gesture towards the stairs.

"I prefer that you learn them from such inquiries as you will make above," said he. "My wife will tell you what she knows about it, and there is a servant or two who may have something to say. I would speak to no one else," he added, with a deepening of the furrow in his brow; "at least not at present. Only,"—and here his manner became markedly impressive,—"understand this. Those diamonds must be found in forty-eight hours, no matter who suffers, or what consequences follow a firm and determined pursuit of them. I will stop at nothing to have them back in the time mentioned, and I do not expect you to. If they are here by Thursday night—" and the hand he held out with its fingers curved and grasping actually trembled with his vehemence—"I will give you five hundred dollars Friday afternoon. If they are here without noise, scandal, or—" his voice sank further—"disquietude to my wife, I will increase the sum to a thousand. Isn't that handsome?" he queried, with an attempt at a lighter tone, which was not altogether successful.

"Very," was my short but deferential reply. And,

interested enough by this time, I turned towards the door, when he stopped me.

"One moment," said he. "I have endeavored not to forestall your judgment by any surmises or conclusions of my own. But, after you have investigated the matter and come to some sort of theory in regard to it, I should like to hear what you have to say."

"I will be happy to consult with you," was my reply; and, seeing that he had no further remarks to offer, I prepared to accompany him up-stairs.

The house was a superb one, and not the least handsome portion of it was the staircase. As we went up, the eye rested everywhere on the richest artistic effects of carved wood-work and tapestry hangings. Nor was the glitter of brass lacking, nor the sensuous glow which is cast by the light striking through ruby-colored glass. At the top was a square hall fitted up with divans and heavily bespread with rugs. At one end a half-drawn portière disclosed a suite of apartments furnished with a splendor equal to that which marked the rest of the house, while at the other was a closed door, towards which Mr. Winchester advanced.

I was hastily following him, when a young man, coming from above, stepped between us. Mr. Winchester at once turned.

"Are you going out?" he asked this person, in a tone that lacked the cordiality of a parent, while it yet suggested the authority of one.

The young gentleman, who was of fine height and carriage, paused with a curious, hesitating air.

"Are you?" he inquired, ignoring my presence, or possibly not noticing it, I being several feet from him and somewhat in the shadow.

"We may show ourselves at the Smiths for a few minutes,

by and by," Mr. Winchester returned.

"No; I am not going out," the young man said, and, turning, he went again up-stairs.

Mr. Winchester's eye followed him. It was only for a moment; but to me, accustomed as I am to note the smallest details in the manner and expression of a person, there was a language in that look which opened a whole field of speculation.

"Your son?" I inquired, stepping nearer to him.

"My wife's son," he replied; and, without giving me an opportunity to put another query, he opened the door before him and ushered me in.

A tall, elegant woman of middle age was seated before the mirror, having the final touches given to her rich toilette by a young woman who knelt on the floor at her side. A marked picture, and this not from the accessories of wealth and splendor everywhere observable, but from the character of the two faces, which, while of an utterly dissimilar cast, and possibly belonging to the two extremes of society, were both remarkable for their force and individuality of expression, as well as for the look of trouble and suppressed anxiety, which made them both like the shadows of one deep, dark thought.

The younger woman was the first to notice us and rise. Though occupying a humble position and accustomed to defer to those around her, there was extreme grace in her movement and a certain charm in her whole bearing which made it natural for the eye to follow her. I did not long allow myself this pleasure, however, for in another instant Mrs. Winchester had caught sight of our forms in the mirror, and, rising with a certain cold majesty, in keeping with her imposing figure and conspicuous if mature beauty, stepped towards us with a slow step, full of repose and quiet determination. Whatever her feelings might be, they were without the fierceness and acrimony which characterized those of her husband. But were they less keen? At first glance I thought not, but at the second I doubted. Mrs. Winchester was already a riddle to me.

"Millicent,"—so her husband addressed her,—"allow me to introduce to you a young man from the police force. If the diamonds are to be recovered before the week is out, he is the man to do it. I pray you offer him every facility for learning the facts. He may wish to speak to the servants and to—" his eye roamed towards the young girl, who, I thought, turned pale under his scrutiny—"to Philippa."

"Philippa knows nothing," the lady's indifferent side-look seemed to say, but her lips did not move, nor did she speak till he had left the room and closed the door behind him. Then she turned to me and gave me first a careless look and then a keener and more sustained one.

"You have been told how I lost my diamonds," she remarked at length.

"They said at the station that a man had entered by your second-story window while you were at dinner."

"Not at dinner," she corrected gravely. "I do not leave my jewel-box lying open, while I go down to dinner. I was in the reception-room below—Mr. Winchester had sent word that he wished to see me for an instant—and being on the point of going to an evening party, my diamonds were in their case on the mantel-piece. When I came back the case was there, but no diamonds. They had been carried off in my absence."

I glanced at the mantel-shelf. On it lay the open jewel-case. "What made you think a burglar took them?" I asked, my eyes on the lady I was addressing, but my ears open to the quick, involuntary drawing in of the breath which had escaped the young girl at the last sentence of her mistress.

"The window was up—I had left it closed—and there

was a sound of scurrying feet on the pavement below. I had just time to see the forms of two men hurrying down the street. You know there have been a series of burglaries of this nature lately."

I bowed, for her imperiousness seemed to demand it. Then I glanced at Philippa. She was standing with her face half averted, trifling with some object on the table, but her apparent unconcern was forced, and her hand trembled so that she hastily dropped the article with which she was toying and turned in such a manner that she hid it as well as her countenance from view.

I made a note of this and allowed my attention to return to Mrs. Winchester.

"At what time was this?" I inquired.

"Seven o'clock."

"Late for a burglary of this kind."

A flush sudden and deep broke out on the lady's cheek.

"It was successful, however," she observed.

Ignoring her anger, which may have arisen from sheer haughtiness and a natural dislike to having any statement she chose to make commented upon, I pursued my inquiries.

"And how long, madam, do you think you were downstairs?"

"Some five minutes or so; certainly not ten."

"And the window was closed when you left the room and open when you returned?"

"I said so."

I glanced at the windows. They were both closed now and the shades drawn.

"May I ask you to show me which window, and also how wide it stood open?"

"It was the window over the stoop, and it stood half-way

open."

I passed at once to the window.

"And the shade?" I asked, turning.

"Was—was down."

"You are sure, madam?"

"Quite; it was by the noise it made as I opened the door that I noticed the window was open."

"Your first glance, then, was not at the mantel-piece?"

"No, sir, but my second was." Her self-possession was almost cold.

This great lady evidently did not enjoy her position of witness, notwithstanding the heavy loss she had sustained, and the fact that the inquisition being made was all in her own interests. I was not to be repelled by her manner, however, for a suspicion had seized me which somewhat accounted for the words and method pursued by Mr. Winchester, and a suspicion once formed, holds imperious sway over the mind of a detective till it is either disproved by facts or confirmed in the same manner into a settled belief.

"Madam," I remarked, "your loss is very great, and demands the most speedy and vigorous effort on the part of the police, that it may not result in a permanent one. Has it struck you"—and I looked firmly at the young girl whom, by my change of position, I had brought again into view—"that it was in any way peculiar that chance thieves working in this dangerous and conspicuous manner should know just the moment to make the hazardous effort which resulted so favorably to themselves? These burglaries which, as you say, have been so plentiful of late, have hitherto all taken place at the hour the family are supposed to be at dinner, while this occurred just when the family would reasonably be supposed to be returning up-stairs. Besides, the gas was burning in this room, was it not?”

“Yes.”

“And the shades down?”

“Yes.”

“So that, till the stoop had been climbed and the room entered, the thief had every reason to believe it was occupied, unless he had notification to the contrary from some one better situated than himself?”

The lady’s eyes opened, and a slight, sarcastic smile parted her lips; but I was not studying her at this moment, but the young Philippa. Humble as she evidently was, and in a condition of mind that caused her to place a restraint upon herself, she took a step forward as I said this, and her mouth opened, as if she would fling some word into the conversation that would neither bear the stamp of humility nor sustain her previous rôle of indifference. But a moment’s thought was sufficient to quell her passionate impulse, and in another instant she was gliding quietly from the room, when I leaned toward Mrs. Winchester and whispered:

“Request the young woman to wait in the hall outside, and suggest that she leave the door open. I do not feel like letting out of my sight just yet any person, no matter how reliable, who has listened to my last remark.”

Mrs. Winchester looked surprised, and eyed me with something of the expression she might have betrayed if I had begged her to stop a mouse from escaping the conference we were holding. But she did what I asked her, and that with a cold, commanding air which proved that, however useful she found the deft and graceful Philippa, she had no real liking for her or any interest in her beyond that which sprang from the value of her services. Was this state of things the fault of Mrs. Winchester or of Philippa? I had not time to determine. The docility of the latter was not, perhaps, to be trusted too far, especially if, as I half suspected, there was some tie between her and the thieves who had carried off Mrs. Winchester's jewels; and while she still lingered where I could see her, I must put the question so evidently demanded by the gravity of the situation.

"Mrs. Winchester," I said, "is there any one in your house whom you think capable of being in league with the robbers?"

The question took her by surprise; she started, and the flush reappeared on her cheek. "I do not understand you," she began; but, speedily recovering her self-possession, she exclaimed, in a low but emphatic tone, "No; how could you think of such a thing? It is the work of professional burglars and of them alone."

I made a slight but unmistakable gesture towards the hall.

"Who is that girl?" I asked.

"Philippa? My maid," she answered, without the slightest token of understanding, much less of sharing, the suspicion which I feared I had, perhaps, too strongly suggested by my rather pointed inquiry. "Or, rather," she corrected, with some slight show of sarcasm, "she is what is commonly called a companion; being sufficiently well educated to read to me if I happen to be in the mood for listening, or even to play on the piano, if music is required in the house."

The chill indifference of this answer stamped Mrs. Winchester as a woman of more elegance than feeling; but as that only made my rather disagreeable task easier, it would be ungracious in me to criticise it.

"How long has she been with you?" I pursued.

"Oh, a year; perhaps more."

"And you know her well; her antecedents and associates?"

"Yes; I know her; all that there is to know. She is not a

deep person, nor is she worthy your questions. Let us drop Philippa."

"In one moment," I returned. "In a case like this I must satisfy myself thoroughly as to the character and past history of all who are in the house. I have seen Philippa, and consequently push my inquiries in her regard first. With whom did she live before she came to you, and where does she spend her time when she is not with you in the house?"

Mrs. Winchester grew visibly impatient. "Follies!" she cried; then, hurriedly, as if anxious to be done with my importunities, "Philippa is the daughter of the clergyman who married my husband and myself. I have always known her; she came from her father's death-bed to my house. As for associates, she has none; and the time she spends out of my rooms is so small that I think it is hardly worth inquiring how or where it is employed. Have you any further inquiries to make?"

I had, but I reserved them. "Will you let me speak to Philippa?" I asked.

Her gesture was one of the utmost disdain, but it contained an acquiescence of which I was not slow in availing myself. Stepping rapidly into the hall, I approached the slight figure I had managed to keep in view during this conversation.

But at my first movement in her direction the young girl started, and before I could address her she had passed through the doorway of the opposite room and disappeared in the darkness beyond.

I immediately stepped back to the lady I had left.

"Do those rooms communicate with a back staircase?" I inquired.

"Yes," she returned, with uncompromising coldness.

I was baffled; that is, as far as Philippa was concerned.

Accepting the situation, however, with what grace I could, I bowed my acknowledgments to Mrs. Winchester, and excusing myself for the moment, went hurriedly below.

I found her husband awaiting me with ill-concealed anxiety.

"Well?" he asked, at my reappearance.

"I have come to a conclusion," said I.

He drew me into a remote corner of the room, where, without our conversation being overheard, he could still keep his eye on the staircase, visible through the half-open door.

"Let me hear," said he.

I at once spoke my mind.

"The thief was no chance one; he not only knew that your house contained diamonds, but he knew where to find them and when. Either a signal was given him when to enter or the diamonds were thrown into his hand out of the window. Does my conviction coincide with yours?"

He smiled a grim smile and waived the question.

"And who do you think gave the signal or threw the diamonds? Do not be afraid to speak names; the case is too serious for paltering."

"Well," said I, "I have been in the house but a few minutes and have seen but three persons besides yourself. I had rather not mention any one as the possible accomplice of so daring a crime till I have seen and conversed with every one here. But there is a girl up-stairs—you yourself called my attention to her—about whom I should like to ask a question or two. I allude to Philippa, Mrs. Winchester's companion."

He turned an eye full of expectancy towards me.

"Do you like her? Have you confidence in her? Is she a person to be trusted?" I inquired.

His glance grew quite bright, and he bowed with almost a gesture of respect.

"You could not have a better witness," he remarked.

The answer was so unexpected, I hastily dropped my eyes.

"She will talk, then, if I interrogate her?" said I.

It was now his turn to look disconcerted.

"Then you have not done so?" he asked.

"I have not had the opportunity," I rejoined.

"Ah," he exclaimed, "I see." And with a look and manner hard to describe, he added, "Mrs. Winchester naturally kept the girl quiet. I might have expected that."

Astonished at this new turn, I ventured to speak the thought suggested by an admission so extraordinary.

"And why should Mrs. Winchester wish to suppress any evidence calculated to lead to the discovery of a thief who had so heavily robbed her?"

The gleam of satisfaction which for the last few moments had lighted up the countenance of the gentleman before me, faded perceptibly.

"I see," he observed, "that our opinions on this matter are less in accord than I supposed. But," he continued more heartily, "you have, as you very justly remarked just now, been but a few minutes in the house, and have not had full opportunity to learn the facts. I will wait till you have talked with Philippa. Shall I call her here?"

"Do," I urged; "she is below, I think, though possibly she may still be in the rooms above;" and I explained how she had started away at my approach, hiding herself in apartments to which I felt I had not the right of access.

He frowned, and moved hastily toward the door, but paused half-way to ask me another question.

"Before I go," said he, "I should like to inquire what word of Mrs. Winchester led you to the conclusion that the theft was committed by some one in the house?"

"Wait," cried I, "you are going too fast; I do not say the theft was committed by some one in the house. I merely speak of an accomplice."

"Who flung the diamonds out of the window—"

"Or merely gave the signal that they were accessible, and for the moment unguarded."

He waved his hand impatiently.

"Let us not waste time," he exclaimed. "I want to know what Mrs. Winchester said—"

"She said nothing," I interrupted, for my haste was as great as his; "that is, nothing beyond the necessary relation of the facts—"

"Which were—"

"That the jewels were lying open in their case on the bureau; that you called her from below; and that she hastened to respond by her presence; was gone five minutes or so, and, returning, found the window open and the diamonds gone. As she had left the window shut, she naturally sprang to it and looked out, in time to see two men hurrying down the street. Surely these facts you know as well as I."

"I was curious," he replied. "So those are the facts you received, and it is from them alone you gathered the conclusion you have stated?"

"No," said I, "there was Philippa."

"But she said nothing."

"I know, but she did not need to speak. I heard her heart beat, if I may so express myself, and from its beatings came the conviction I have given you."

Mr. Winchester bestowed upon me an approving smile.

"You are all I thought you," was his comment. "Philippa's heart did beat, and with most unwonted emotions, too. Philippa saw the person who relieved Mrs. Winchester of her jewels."

"What!" I cried, "and you—"

He did not wait to hear the end of my remonstrance. "I say so," he went on, "because while Mrs. Winchester was here, and before she ascended, I saw Philippa go up. She had just time to reach the head of the stairs, when the person whose step I had already detected crossing the floor above, gained the hall—"

"The hall?" I cried.

"Yes. Can it be you really allowed yourself to dream for a moment that the thief who stole this small fortune came in by the window?"

"Mr. Winchester," said I, "when I left the police station it was with some doubt, I confess, as to whether this theft had been committed in just the way the man who brought your note said it had been. But after hearing what Mrs. Winchester had to say—"

"Mrs. Winchester's account of this occurrence is not to be depended upon," he broke in calmly, but determinedly. "Shall I give you a fact or two? The window which my wife declares she found open when she went up-stairs was not raised while she was down here, but after her return, for I heard it. The step which crossed the floor above us while we were talking together here, went out, not by any window, but by the door leading into the hall; so that—"

"Mr. Winchester," I interrupted, "do you realize that if what you say is true, the diamonds are probably still in your house?"

"Just where I think they are, Mr. Byrd; just where I

think they are."

I began to have a strong notion of his suspicion.

"And Philippa," I suggested.

"Saw what I heard."

I made no further effort to detain him. "Let us have her here," I cried. "If what you surmise is true, the mystery ought to be one of easy solution. So easy," I could not forbear adding, "that I wonder you felt the need of sending for a detective."

"You forget," he observed, "that it is not so much the discovery of the thief I am after, as the recovery of the jewels. The former I might have managed without your assistance; but the latter requires an authority backed by the law." And merely stopping to call my attention to the necessity of keeping a watch on the front door that no one should escape from the house while he was gone, he hastily left me and went up-stairs.

He was absent some twenty minutes, during which I heard him pass in and out of his wife's room. But when he came down he was alone, and his countenance, which before had looked merely anxious and determined, now bore the marks of anger and impatience.

"I do not know by what motive she is actuated," cried he, "but I cannot induce Philippa to speak. She insists she has nothing to say."

"You saw her, then? I was afraid she had escaped by the back-stairs."

"Hardly," was the dry retort. "I caused the door leading to the rear hall to be locked long ago."

I bowed in admiration of his caution.

"No one can pass from the upper to the lower portion of this house without going by this door; how else could I be sure the diamonds had not already been smuggled out of the building?"

"And you are positively sure that, as it is, they are still here."

"Positively."

"And that Philippa, although she will not speak, knows who took the jewels, or at least who it was that entered the room above while Mrs. Winchester was down here?"

"Yes."

"Then," I declared, "our coast is clear. To find the diamonds it is only necessary to search the house, and as for the culprit, Philippa will find it difficult to keep silence when once the law has taken its course, and duty as well as honor compels her to speak."

He nodded and stood a moment thinking.

"You would search the house?" he repeated at last. "It is a large house and its places of concealment innumerable; I do not think we should recover them by that means—not in the time I have specified. Listen to my plan. Mrs. Winchester and myself expected to go to a certain reception to-night. It is a grand affair, and it is desirable that we should be present. We will go there, but before going I will make it known throughout the house that you are a detective, and say that it is your intention to search the house for the missing jewels as soon as you can get the necessary assistance from your office. This will alarm the guilty, and if I am not very much mistaken, lead to the endeavor of some one person in this house to leave it. If this should prove true, do not hinder the attempt, for that person will have the diamonds in his possession, and if followed, as you will take measures he shall be, their recovery must be a matter of an hour or two; for a man is more easily searched than a house."

"An admirable scheme," I exclaimed, wondering at

an acumen I certainly should not have looked for in the wealthy broker. "I see but one flaw in it. If Mrs. Winchester heard that her house was to be ransacked in her absence, would she consent to go to the reception?"

"Mrs. Winchester will be in her carriage when I make the announcement. I shall certainly see to that."

"Very well, then," said I, "it only remains for me to procure from the police-station the man I want for the pursuit you mention."

"I will call there on my way to the reception with any note you may choose to write."

I scribbled two names on a card.

"Either of those men will answer," said I. "Let him take his station in the area next to this, and when posted there give the call. He will understand. Will the guilty person be likely to lead him a long chase?"

"That it is as impossible for me to know as you. I have no conception where the thief will go upon leaving this house. To some place favorable for the concealment of his booty, of course, but where, time and the skill of his pursuer must determine."

"I will just add a line of caution to that pursuer," said I, and taking the card I scribbled a few directions on its back, after which I gave it to Mr. Winchester.

In exchange he handed me two keys.

"This one unlocks the door leading to the back-stairs, and this the front door of the basement." After which explanation he left me, and in another moment I heard him go up-stairs and enter his wife's room.

The programme we had agreed upon was carried out to the letter. In less than a half hour Mr. and Mrs. Winchester came down, he looking pale and stern, she haughty and imperturbably calm. The carriage, which I had heard drive up a moment before, stood at the door and they passed immediately out, but not before I had time to observe that she wore the same dress I had seen her in above, a rich mauve-colored velvet made high in the throat and heavily loaded with what I believe they call a passementerie of pearl beads enriched with lace; a species of garniture which in my eyes obviated the necessity of any further adornment more pretentious than the simple cluster of pearls she wore in her ears.

"A noble and a dignified presence," I thought as she passed, and wondered if the heart under that violet robe beat any faster than her appearance betokened, or whether she was indeed one of that class of women in whom the ills and exigences of life stir but faint chords and produce but slight emotions.

The bang of the carriage door was followed by the almost immediate reappearance of Mr. Winchester.

"Now," said he, "to business!" And looking up the stairs, he hailed, with a glance of satisfaction, the descending figure of the young man whom we had before met on the landing above, and whom he had designated to me as his wife's son.

"Ah, Lawrence," said he, "come down. I sent for you and Miss Irwin—by the by, where is she? Oh, I see, looking over the banisters above—that I might introduce to you Mr. Byrd, a detective from the police force, whose business here, as you may judge, is to recover for us your mother's diamonds. It is necessary for you to know him, for he, as well as myself, has come to the conclusion that your mother is mistaken in believing that the jewels were stolen by some one entering from without. Indeed, he is sure that not only is the thief a member of this household, but that the diamonds are still on the premises, and can be found by a thorough and systematic search. He is, therefore, going to take advantage of your mother's absence to put his theory to the test, and as soon as suitable assistance can be procured from the police station, will begin a search that will stop at no receptacles, be balked by no place of concealment, however personal or private. I say this, because I do not wish you or Miss Irwin to feel irritated if he is obliged to enter your rooms, there being, as you know, one or two old servants with us whose feelings might justly be wounded if their persons or belongings were subjected to an examination that was not shared in by every individual in the house. You will, therefore, be ready with your keys, and, by setting an example to the servants, make the efforts of this officer as light as possible. Am I understood, Lawrence?"

"Certainly, sir."

The answer was as nonchalant as the question, which was put with an easy and light good-nature, calculated to deceive every ear but that of a detective. Indeed Mr. Lawrence Sutton—I learned his name afterwards—seemed to be awakening from a dream—and the moment his step-father was gone,—for Mr. Winchester did not linger after saying the above,—he turned and went immediately up-stairs just as if I had not been standing there.

His conduct was so unexpected, I paused, irresolute. This was the man Mr. Winchester suspected, I felt sure, and here he was going, for aught I knew, straight to the spot where the valuable articles lay concealed whose recovery and delivery into Mr. Winchester's hands would bring me what I was fain to consider in these days of my poverty, a small fortune. Should I follow him, or should I trust to Mr. Winchester's judgment and wait for him to re-descend? The conviction that I would only defeat my own ends by surprising him too soon, decided me at last to remain below, and, withdrawing into the reception-room, I waited, with indescribable anxiety, first for the peculiar call which would notify me that my colleague had arrived on the scene, and, secondly, for the returning step of Mr. Sutton. But before either of these sounds assailed my ears there came another which aroused my keenest curiosity. This was a noise of whispering on the floor above, followed by a short, sharp cry of joy in a voice I felt sure belonged to the young gentleman I had seen. Then all was silence, during which came the call without, then a rush above as of hurrying feet, after which I heard no more till—yes, the eagerly expected sound of a descending step awakened all my energies, and glancing through the crack of the door near which I stood, I saw Mr. Sutton coming down with his overcoat on.

More satisfied than I could say, not at this evidence of the truth of Mr. Winchester's suspicions,—for Mr. Sutton had a fine air and a countenance which, if it bore the unmistakable signs of a life of dissipation, had yet an expression that was not without its attraction,—but at the result of an experiment which was almost daring in its nature, I waited to hear the front door open and close. But I had not calculated on Mr. Sutton being a gentleman of great courtesy and many resources, and before I was fully aware of his presence, he was at my side, bowing with extreme urbanity, and holding out a chain from which I saw several keys hanging.

"Mr. Winchester has requested me to give you these. By their aid you will be enabled to open every box and drawer that I own. As for the others, you must find your own way of entrance and examination. I have an important engagement out which will keep me, perhaps, an hour. On my return I will lend you all the assistance I can; for I am naturally as anxious as any one that so valuable a treasure as my mother's diamonds should not be lost to the family."

I bowed and he drew back, taking out a pair of new

gloves, which, to my unbounded astonishment, he stopped to fit on with great nicety and precision. Then he moved towards the door, but even there he paused and looked up the stairs before finally putting on his hat and going out.

"A consummate actor!" thought I, and sprang to the window, through which I rather incautiously peered. He was descending the steps, still slowly, but with more of an air of determination than he had shown within. In another moment he was on the side-walk, and in an instant later was walking rapidly down the street. Hurrying from the window, I went to the front door and opened it. A man was leaving the area next door, and, before I turned to come in, I had the satisfaction of seeing Mr. Sutton's tall form closely shadowed by the most knowing and discreet assistant we have on the force.

"Now for hours of dreary patience," mused I, sinking into a large easy chair near a table of inviting-looking books.

But scarcely had I uttered this thought than I sprang to my feet in fresh excitement. Another step was on the stair, another presence in the room.

Turning in the full expectation of seeing Miss Irwin, I encountered the gaze of an old and feeble woman. Surprised, I bowed with respect; upon which she immediately said:

"I hear that Mr. Winchester has decided to have a search made through the house for the diamonds that Mrs. Winchester has lost. Is it going to be done to-night?"

"It will have to be done to-night if at all," I returned with pardonable prevarication. "There would be but little satisfaction in undertaking it after any communication had been established between its inmates and the world without."

"Then," said she, with little or no heed to the latter part of my sentence, "may I ask as a favor that you will make it convenient to go through my room first? I am Mrs.

Winchester's aunt; and I am sure she would not wish me to be kept out of my bed any later than is necessary. My room is small and—"

Poor old lady! it was really cruel. I made haste to relieve her mind.

"There can be no necessity for searching your room—" I began.

But she interrupted me with prompt decision.

"You are mistaken," said she. "If there is a room in this house which ought to be looked into, it is mine. For the very reason that it is the last one a detective would examine, makes it possibly the very one a thief would choose for the purpose of concealment. I prefer you to go through my room, sir."

I was astonished and not a little perplexed. The old lady looked so determined it was evident she was not to be trifled with. But I was not ready to explain to her that the threatened search was but a ruse de guerre, which had already produced its desired result; and yet, if I did not do so, how was I to account for a delay that would inconvenience her so materially? I could see but one way out of the difficulty, and that was to make a superficial examination of her room and her effects, after which I would proclaim myself satisfied with my scrutiny, in the hope that she would be so too. I accordingly answered her that I appreciated her position perfectly, and that if she would consent to it, I would go to her apartment at once.

She signified that she would be only too happy; whereupon I immediately led the way up-stairs. She followed me up the two flights, and earnestly pointed out the door of her room. But as I approached it I heard a suspicious sound on the floor below, and looking over the banisters, beheld the lithe and agile figure of Philippa gliding down the stairs to the front door. She was dressed for the street, and had evidently taken advantage of my position to escape from the house.

Instantly a throng of doubts and suspicions passed through my mind. I was the victim of a plot, and the old lady was neither so innocent nor so disinterested as she appeared. When she persuaded me to go up-stairs it was with the direct intention of giving Philippa the opportunity to reach the street unhindered. I knew it even before I noticed how her feeble and panting form filled the narrow passage at the head of the stairs, necessitating some slight rudeness on my part to pass her. But rudeness, even to an aged and decrepit lady, was of small account in an exigency like this. Twenty-five thousand dollars were in all probability slipping from my grasp, to say nothing of my reputation as an astute and not readily deceived detective. And yet, was it now and in this way the diamonds were leaving the house, or had they already been carried away, as I formerly believed, by Mr. Sutton? Either might be true, or, as I had time to think before I was half-way down the first flight, neither might be true. His departure, and now hers, might be equally a ruse to withdraw attention from the house and the real concealer of these valuable gems; and, pausing just one instant in my descent, I looked back at the place where I had left the old lady tottering from the push I had been obliged to give her in my anxiety to pass. She was standing there still, but the look with which she followed me was one of ill-concealed satisfaction, and though she drew back at my first glance, I had time to observe that a smile had crept into the corners of her mouth that augured poorly for the success of any design that I might entertain.

Meanwhile Philippa's hand was on the knob of the front door, and she would have been out of the house in another instant if she had not stopped to glance at the hat rack, with the deliberate purpose, as I believe, of hindering me in my pursuit by appropriating my hat if it hung there.

But fortunately for me I had carried it with me into the reception-room, so her glance as well as her delay was but momentary. Before I was well at the top of the first flight I heard the front door close, and knew I had to decide in a breath, as it were, whether to follow her and so forsake the building and it might be the very gems I was seeking to recover, or to allow her to go her way unhindered, in face of the equal possibility of her bearing them away to some place of safer concealment.

The thought of Mr. Winchester decided me instantly. If I failed in recovering the gems by following Philippa, I would but lose my reward and possibly a little of my prestige as a detective; but if I failed in the same undertaking by not following her, Mr. Winchester would have the right to reproach me with a manifest disregard of his orders. For had he not said, "Watch who it is who endeavors to leave this house after your threat to search it, and follow him, for that person will have the diamonds." To be sure Mr. Sutton had already gone and was being followed, but if a dozen left after him, especially after resorting to subterfuge to elude pursuit, would it not be my duty to see that they were also followed and that with the same care and circumspection I had thought proper to have employed in his case? There could be no doubt on the matter; so flinging all other consideration to the winds, I gave myself up to the pursuit of this flying sprite, closing the front door after me without a suspicion but that my first glance down the street would show me in what direction she had started.

But neither my glances down the street nor up revealed to me Philippa, and agitated by my first fear that I had possibly undertaken more than I could accomplish, I dashed down to the corner, which was that of Madison Avenue, and looking hastily this way and that, saw on the block below the supple and delicate form of a female which I had barely decided was hers, when a car stopped and she stepped aboard and was carried away before I could get breath to cry stop! to the rather obtuse conductor who assisted her.

Happily the next car was not many blocks off, and when I boarded it and found the driver a man I knew, I felt that the case was not so hopeless as first appeared. With but little persuasion he consented to urge the horses on a little faster than the schedule called for, so that in a few minutes we had drawn up close enough to the car in front for me to see each figure as it descended. In this way I was enabled to follow Miss Irwin with more satisfaction than if I had got into the same car with her; and as her ride was short, I soon was stepping lightly behind her down Forty-fifth Street. She did not walk two blocks before she stopped, ran up a stoop, rang the bell and was admitted.

I hastened quickly after her, looked at the number and paused confounded. Why, this was a house I well knew; one which many people visited,—though not often on the same errand as Miss Irwin, I must believe,—one which I had sometimes visited myself; the home of the well-known minister, Mr. Randall.

Nonplussed for the moment, I stood hesitating, when to add to my astonishment a man stepped up to me from behind, and tapping me familiarly on the back, said:

"Well, what do you make of it?"

It was Hawkins.

"What! you here?" I exclaimed.

"Certain!" he cried, "and my man, too."

It was inexplicable. Fortunately there was hope of solving the mystery.

"I think I will go in," said I. "I know Mr. Randall quite well. If one or both of them come out before I do, follow. I will not be gone any longer than is necessary."

He nodded and fell back into his hiding-place. I rang the

bell and asked for Mr. Randall.

"He is busy just now, sir," explained the neat servant girl who answered my summons. "But if you will step into his study, he will soon be ready to see you."

I needed no second invitation. In a few moments I was ensconced in the cosy back parlor, listening to the low murmur of voices that came from the room in front through the heavy folding-doors that separated the two apartments. Of these voices I could distinguish two; the heavy bass of Mr. Randall, and the lighter, smoother tones of the young man who had brought me his keys in Seventy-third Street. Suddenly both voices ceased, and there was a slight bustle, then a solemn silence, then—could it be the sound of Mr. Randall's voice again, not in the conversational tone he had previously used, but in the measured accent he was accustomed to use in the pulpit. "The enigma increases," thought I, and, regardless of appearances, I crept to the folding-doors and glued my ear against the narrow crack that marked their line of division. What I heard only increased my curiosity to the fever point. At all risks, and in despite of all ordinary proprieties, I must see whom the clergyman was addressing; so, exerting all my skill and no little of the caution of a professional detective, I pried the doors the least bit apart and saw,—what I certainly had not come there to see, and yet a very pretty sight for all that—Mr. Sutton and Philippa Irwin kneeling before Mr. Randall, and that gentleman pronouncing over them the marriage benediction.

There was another lady and two gentlemen in a group about them, but beyond noting that the lady was Mrs. Randall, and the gentlemen members of the same family, I did not bestow a thought upon them, my whole attention being given to the man and woman, whom I had been following under so sinister a suspicion, only to find myself a witness of the most serious act of their lives.

The surprise of the occasion and the touching nature of the whole scene, made me for the instant forget the diamonds and what my very presence in that spot implied. But, when the final words had been said, and the few congratulations offered, the young people faced about and I caught a glimpse of the bride's countenance, I remembered with a shock the gloomy nature of the shadow which surrounded them; and while I could not help but give my sympathy to a condition of things at once so novel and so interesting, I also felt my determination as a detective return. For Philippa's face wore not the look of a happy bride, but that of a woman who has just dared everything that some cherished scheme might be fulfilled or some dreadful ill averted. Indeed, there was terror in the eye with which she regarded her husband; a terror so mixed with love and the light of something like hope as she met his glance of triumphant satisfaction, that I felt I must probe the matter of the diamonds to the bottom if only to solve the mystery of her action, and the motives by which she had been governed in this gift of herself at a moment so manifestly unpropitious to happiness and honor.

Meanwhile, Mr. Randall was saying some words of courtesy and farewell, and, seeing that in another moment his steps might be turned in my direction, I pushed to the doors at which I was standing, with even a greater caution than that with which I had separated them, and falling back to my old station on the sofa, I awaited with equal interest and impatience his entrance and the sound of the young couple's departure.

Mr. Randall appeared and the front door closed at the same time. Resigning Mr. Sutton and his bride to the care of the man without, I turned my attention to the clergyman. I knew enough of his character and life to be certain he had not married them without knowing something of their history and condition, and that knowledge I meant to have.

Some of my readers may not need to be told that I, Horace Byrd, was not always on the detective force; that I had had my bringing up in different circles, and that I was by birth and education what is called a gentleman. I speak of this here to account for the affability with which Mr. Randall greeted me, and his readiness to satisfy what, under ordinary circumstances, might have been considered a most impertinent and inexcusable curiosity. He was my father's friend, and he listened with respect while I made my excuses, and opened at once upon the subject that occupied my thoughts.

"Mr. Randall," said I, "the errand with which I approach you is of a most singular nature. The couple you have just married—pardon me, my ears are good and my presence here is in connection with that same couple—lie under a suspicion of wrong-doing that may or may not lead to consequences of the most serious nature. What that wrong-doing is I had rather not state, since it is as yet merely a suspicion from which they may be able to clear themselves. But what I will say is, that you will be furthering their welfare and assisting at the unravelment of a most mysterious occurrence if you will tell me what you know about them, and the causes which led to this evidently hasty and clandestine marriage."

"I am greatly astonished," were his first words; "and feel strongly inclined to ask you what these poor young folks could have done beyond loving each other and marrying in despite of the pride and ambitious projects of Mr. and Mrs. Winchester. But curiosity pure and simple is unworthy of a clergyman, so I will merely say if they are doing or have done anything that could be called really wrong I was in complete ignorance of it, and that their marriage is but

the culmination of an intention long known to me if not
to the world and that society to which the groom if not the
bride belongs.”

“Now,” returned I, “you astonish me. They were engaged,
then, and you knew it; something which I can scarcely
believe his own mother did.”

“Very likely,” was the quiet retort. “Mrs. Winchester is
not one whom a proud man would take into his confidence
if he meant to make what is called a poor and unequal
match.”

“Still,” I began—

“Still,” he interrupted, “a son should show a certain
consideration and respect to the mother who bore him
and who always has displayed, as he himself declares,
forbearance to his faults and sympathy for the weakness
that caused them. I know all this,” Mr. Randall continued,
“and I agree with you in your opinion; but there were
certain peculiarities in this special case which offer at
least some excuse for his action and my sympathy with
it. Lawrence Sutton was not always a respectable member
of society. He was a wild boy, an extravagant youth, and a
more than dissipated man. His mother loved him but could
not control him, powerful and determined spirit though she
is. Nor had his step-father’s position and enormous wealth
any influence in controlling passions that partook almost
of the recklessness of the foreign fast society amongst
which he was more or less unfortunately cast. He seemed
to be without aspiration, and yet he was not shallow, nor
ungenerous, nor mean. His mother, whose thoughts few
can penetrate, looked on and was silent; his step-father,
who had not nature to help him to a consideration for his
faults, showed his anger and threatened to show him his
door but never did. He lived an outcast from the best and
showed no prospect of amendment till suddenly—it was

a year ago—the greatest and most startling change took place in his habits and general style of living; and from being a careless man about town, he became the courteous, careful gentleman, alive to the place of honor he had lost in society and active in his endeavor to regain it. His mother, always hopeful for her boy, naturally attributed to her own quiet influence and unbroken faith this wonderful restoration to manhood and honor: but I knew better; I to whom human nature has been an open book for twenty-five years, knew that something fresher and more ideal than any influence Mrs. Winchester was capable of exerting had led this young man to reject a course which had become almost a second nature to him.

"Frequent and prolonged visits at Mr. Winchester's house did not serve to explain the mystery to me. I found Mr. Sutton sitting with the family,—something which I had not seen him do for years,—but how was I to connect this fact with the presence now and then of the quiet young woman, without any special attraction, whom Mrs. Winchester once rather carelessly introduced to me as Miss Irwin; and yet this girl with the subdued look and meek, almost humble aspect, was the force which had acted on this man's nature and turned its impulses, as it were, completely about. To him she was the manifestation of all that was ideal and desirable in womanhood; and from the first moment he saw her, as he afterwards told me, he made up his mind to win her for his wife if it cost him all and every indulgence of his hitherto much to be reprobated life. That he cherished this hope in his heart and did not make a confidant of either of his parents is not to be wondered at. Mrs. Winchester looks upon Philippa as a dependent; a being too insignificant to be regarded, much less admired or feared. Nothing, not even the change in her son's moral life, would ever have convinced her that this girl possessed influence; or if by any means that belief was forced upon her, that it arose from any merit or powers she was bound to acknowledge or respect. A handsome, elegant, worldly-wise woman herself, she sees no excellence that is not linked to those qualities, and would rather, I verily believe, have seen her son thrown back into his old course than owe his redemption to a source so insignificant in appearance and out of all accord with her own views of what was in keeping with her son's prospects and her own social position.

"At least, this is the judgment I have formed of her, and this the explanation which young Sutton gave me of his conduct, in an interview he held with me some six months ago. 'She'—that is, his mother—'shall know nothing of what Philippa is to me till she sees her at my side as my wife,' was his remark to me at that time. 'And that I look to you to make her,' he continued, 'when by perseverance and a proper probation I have induced this pure and uncontaminated being to trust me with her fate and make me what I now believe I am capable of becoming, a man of purpose, ambition, and social standing.'

"Such hopes, such resolution, and such spirit in a man of his type and with his record could not but enlist my sympathy. A soul which I had long thought lost had found its motive to better things, and though this motive was not the highest, it was high enough to give hope for the continuance of the good work to the end of all I could fondly wish for him. I therefore entered into his plans with cordial interest, and though I deprecated his taking any serious step without at least acquainting his mother with his intentions, I promised and have kept my word, that when he came to me with Philippa I would marry them, trusting to his own sense of propriety and her discretion, that the event would be for the honor and happiness of the family as well as for their own mutual joy and satisfaction. But what you tell me now disturbs me where I never thought to be disturbed. They are under suspicion of some evil—what,

I cannot imagine—and you know it; which means that it is flagrant, and possibly makes them amenable to the law."

I did not answer this, for I was full of thoughts. Could it be that this pure and touching story of seemingly true love was destined to be besmirched by the shadow of crime? Had Lawrence Sutton taken the diamonds, and did Philippa Irwin know it; or was Mrs. Winchester's story correct, and the deed one of the common order of burglary?

"What adds to my concern," the good clergyman went on, after waiting a suitable time for me to speak, "is that some folks think—some members of his own family in fact—that the change in his nature, to which I allude, is not so thorough as I have made you understand. They insist that he still carries on his old practices, but more secretly. And they have a reason for this; for whereas, at one time, that is, in the beginning of his acquaintance with Philippa, he used to remain at home during the evening, he has for some months now confined his attentions in that quarter to Sunday night merely, going out as regularly after dinner as he used to do in his wildest days of dissipation. Only he does not come home intoxicated any more, and his eyes, which once looked bleared and heavy, are now clear and wide-awake. I—I wish we knew where he is accustomed to spend his nights."

"Well, we will find out," I assured him, getting up and moving towards the door; "and though I fear the result may not be all we could wish, I will remember your anxiety and relieve as much of it as is possible to-morrow. I must say good-night, now, for this matter is not one that will keep." And merely pausing to thank him for his goodness, I left Mr. Randall and proceeded directly back to the house of Mr. Winchester.

My reflections on the way there were not of a wholly satisfactory nature. If Mr. Sutton and his bride were in possession of the diamonds, there was no telling what they would do or where they would go; separate, possibly, and thus put Hawkins at his wits' end as to which of the two to follow. If they were not in possession of the diamonds, I fully believed I should find them at the house before me. But that was a contingency only satisfactory to my sympathy; for, if the gems were not with them, where were they? Not in Mr. Winchester's house by this time; of that I could be perfectly sure.

So it was with anything but a light heart that I rang the bell this time, and greeting Mr. Winchester's countenance as before, entered again into this dwelling of mystery.

"We have come back," were his hurried words, uttered with feverish intensity. "And you? Have you got the diamonds?"

I shook my head and hastened after him into the reception-room.

"But you followed him? You know where he is? And Philippa? What took her out, too?"

"Wait," I said, "have they come back?"

"Who? Lawrence and Philippa?"

"Yes."

"No."

"I fear they will not come, then," said I.

"They? Why do you associate Lawrence's name with Philippa's?"

I was spared the answer. At that instant I heard the well-known call of my colleague without, and simultaneously with this encouraging sound, the click of the night-key in the door proclaiming the return of Mr. Sutton.

"No," cried I, "here they are; and as I am sure they will have something to say to you which it would embarrass them to utter before a stranger, I will just step out of sight for the moment." And making a dash for the portière behind me, I pulled it aside and stepped into the darkness beyond.

Mr. Winchester made no effort to stop me; he was too much astonished at the sight of his step-son entering with Philippa on his arm. And I, who, without calculation, had stumbled into the first refuge I espied, was equally surprised, not at what I saw, but at the quarters in which I found myself; for the portière, instead of shutting off a room, shielded a closet, and it was amongst a litter of bric-à-brac and old pictures that I now drew myself up, prepared to listen and to see, since this was all that was left to my indiscretion.

"Father,"—it was Mr. Sutton who spoke,—"will you call mother down? There is something I wish to say to her before I take another step in this house."

"But—but no matter about your mother," came in Mr. Winchester's hasty and now deeply agitated tones. "If you have the diamonds, give them to me; give them to me quickly, and nothing more shall ever be said about them. I am not hard on young folks, and—"

"The diamonds? I know nothing about the diamonds," the other broke in, with an impatience that was more startling than anger would have been. "What I wish to say is on a wholly different subject." And I judge that he turned with a look towards Philippa, for the old man's voice became quite shrill as he cried:

"What do you want to say? That you and Philippa are friends? That she did not see you come out of your mother's room two minutes before the diamonds were missed? That you are a saint and every one knows it, and she—"

"Stop!"

Was that the voice of a man stained by the meanest of crimes? I pushed aside the portière and looked out. He was standing like a statue of wrath between Mr. Winchester and the glowing, brilliant, almost transformed Philippa.

"When you speak of her," cried he, letting his hand fall on her arm, with the pride of triumphant possession, "you are speaking of my wife."

Mr. Winchester fell slowly back. It was the only surprise, perhaps, that could have taken his mind off the diamonds.

"Your wife," he repeated, and his eyes slowly traveled to Philippa's face, as if he found it difficult to take in a statement so unexpected.

Mr. Sutton took advantage of the moment to step to the foot of the stairs.

"Mother!" he called, "will you come here?"

She was already in the hall as he, doubtless, perceived, for he hastened back and took Philippa by the hand, and was standing thus when the stately woman crossed the threshold in all the splendor of the rich garments I have hitherto endeavored to describe.

"My son!" was her first startled exclamation, quickly followed by an indescribable murmur, as she saw whom he held by the hand, and noted the fervor of that clasp, and the expression with which he regarded her. "What does this mean?" she asked at length, her hauteur battling with an anger that was yet new, but terrible in its promise of growth.

"Happiness, I hope," was the steady reply. "If not, it at least means a better life on my part and a less humble and dependent one on hers. We are married, mother, and it is my wish—"

He did not finish; at that word married, the haughty woman, struck in the full pride of her hopes and ambitious projects, tottered, and before help could reach her, fell, laying her gray but queenly head at the feet of her whom an hour back she would have scorned to associate with herself in any higher connection than she did the inanimate objects that surrounded her and ministered to her comfort.

There was a rush, a hurried murmur, a pause, then a sudden cry so fraught with wonder and yet so surcharged with triumph, that I could scarcely believe it proceeded from Mr. Winchester's lips, till a sudden swaying in the bended form of Philippa revealed to me Mrs. Winchester lying with the neck of her dress thrown back, and on the throat thus displayed, a glistening cordon of gems which by their brilliancy and size could only be the famous and costly ones for which we had been seeking.

It was the culmination of the evening's surprises.

"The diamonds, the diamonds!" exclaimed Mr. Winchester, and regardless of the still insensible condition of his wife, he stooped and dragged them from her neck, and stood holding them out and looking at them, as if he could hardly credit his good fortune.

As for Mr. Sutton and Philippa, they gave one startled glance at the jewels, another at each other, and then set about restoring their mother.

I was the most thoroughly overcome of them all.

It took some few minutes to bring Mrs. Winchester back to consciousness. Meanwhile, I employed myself in looking at her husband. He had by this time thrust the gems into his pocket, and was gazing at her with a half-sinister, half-pitying glance. But at the first movement on her part he was all attention to her, while, on the contrary, Mr. Sutton and Philippa drew back as if they dreaded to meet her unclosing eye. They might well feel so; it was terrible, and so was her gesture, as, rising from the sofa on which she had been laid, she looked about on them all. But suddenly, and before she could speak, she felt the wind on her throat, and, lifting her hand to it, a great change passed over her.

"Who—who has presumed—" she began; but here she caught her husband's eye, and losing her self-possession, felt around for a chair and fell into it.

"If you are looking for your jewels," that husband remarked, "I have them. It was a curious freak to wear them under instead of over your dress, and then to forget where you had put them and imagine them stolen."

She lifted one thin, white hand as if in protest, but her regal spirit seemed broken, and her eyes filled with something like tears.

"Lawrence!" she exclaimed brokenly, "what have I not done for you! and this is how you repay me."

"Mother," said the young man, with a closer grip of Philippa's hand, "could you ask for any better repayment than the regenerate life I offer you? A year ago I was the shame and disgrace of this family; a man for whom the world had scorn and you only a pitying forbearance. To-day I can walk the streets and drop my eyes before no man's glance; I am a man again, and this—this dear woman is the cause. Is it not enough to make you overlook the trifling disadvantages which annoy your pride but cannot affect your heart?"

But Mrs. Winchester's nature was not one to be touched by any such appeal as this. Indeed, it seemed to restore some of her former hauteur.

"Your mother's love was then insufficient to recall you to a sense of what you owed yourself and her? My sacrifices, my sympathy, my endeavors to uphold you in face of the disapprobation of the whole world were as nothing to you. You had to wait till a puny girl smiled upon you, a waiting-woman, a—"

"Mother," broke in the son, this time with severity in his tone, "Philippa is a lady; she is, moreover, my wife, and so of equal social station with yourself. Let us not be bitter but thankful. For me, an angel has stepped into my life."

It was not wise, but when was love ever wise? Mrs. Winchester's face hardened, and a reckless smile broke out on her lips.

"An angel that has brought ruin to me," said she. "What confidence do you suppose there can henceforth be between my husband and myself since he has found I can deceive him, and deceive him for you?"

"For me?"

"Yes; you can play with my heart, trifle with my pride, marry my waiting-maid before my eyes, never asking whence came the freedom which enables you to do all these things, or what price your mother is paying for the sins her forbearance was not sufficient to make you regret and forsake."

"Mother, what do you mean? I do not understand you at all. What price have you been paying for sins of mine?"

She smiled ironically.

"It is time you showed some curiosity on the subject." Then, with a side glance at her husband, full of bitterness and despair, she went on: "Did you ever ask yourself where the money came from with which I paid your debts two years ago, in Paris?"

"No—that is, I supposed, of course, it came out of your own pocket. Mr. Winchester is a rich man—"

"And I, his wife, must therefore be a rich woman. Well, I may be; but even rich women do not always have a hundred thousand francs at their disposal; and that sum I gave you, and you took from me. Where do you think I obtained it? Not from him, as his face only too plainly testifies."

"Where, then, mother—where, then? Tell me, for I—"

But Mr. Winchester had taken a step forward, and his face was very white.

"Let her answer my questions," said he. "You gave your son, that scapegrace, a hundred thousand francs, two years ago, in Paris?"

She bowed her head, trembling with something more than wrath.

"It was a great sum," he continued, "a great sum! I do not wonder you hesitated to ask me for it. He would never have got it, never. I wonder that you found any friend willing to throw so much money to the dogs."

"It was not a friend," she murmured. "O William!" she went on, with almost a pleading sound in her voice, "we have never had any children, and you do not know what it is to love a son. To see him in peril, disgrace, or necessity, and not seek to relieve him, is impossible. You must make allowances for a mother's heart."

"But this money—these thousands—where did they come from, where?"

She flushed, and her head drooped, but her natural haughtiness soon lifted it again. Rising, she asked, in her turn—

"Mr. Winchester, why did you send for me to-night, as I was dressing for the reception, and, after inquiring if I were going to wear my diamonds, say it was your pleasure that I should do so, and then add, that you wished to borrow them of me to-morrow as you desired to show them to a dealer?"

"Why? because—" It was his turn to flush now—"because I do wish to show them to a dealer."

"And what has a dealer to do with my diamonds?"

"Nothing—a freak of mine. I took a notion to find out just what they were worth."

"And don't you know?" Her voice was very low, her eyes burned on his face.

"Only approximately, madam, approximately."

The glance she had fixed on him, fell. She took a step nearer, but did not speak at once.

"What is it?" he cried. "Why do you hesitate to answer my questions?"

"William," said she, "were it not more to the point to ask why I, who have always been considered an honorable woman, should resort to the subterfuge of stealing my own jewels in order to escape the delivery of them up into other hands?"

"Perhaps," he muttered; "but we will not go into that. No woman enjoys parting with such gems as these even for a few days."

She laughed. "But a woman does not resort to crime, run the risk of police investigation and submit to such indignities as are inflicted upon her by the so-called detective agent, for the mere sake of retaining in her possession jewels of any price. She must have another motive—a motive of terror lest an evil greater than these should come upon her—the loss of her husband's love or trust, the—the—"

"Madam, what have you been doing? What secret underlies all these words?"

"A little one; only a little one. William, do you intend showing that necklace to a dealer to-morrow?"

"Yes, to ascertain its value."

"You had better not."

"Why?"

"Because he would laugh in your face. William, the gems are false—false; there is not a diamond amongst them; only glass, worthless glass!"

He stared at her incredulously; he tore the jewels from his pocket and held them up to the light. Their flash and brilliance seemed to reassure him.

"You are making sport of me, madam. See how they sparkle and throw back the light. Only diamonds shine like that. You do not wish me to take them away from you. Perhaps you fear you may lose them permanently."

"I tell you they are false," she insisted. "I had the exchange made in Paris. I received a hundred thousand francs and these imitations for the necklace. Had not the man who manufactured them been an expert, do you suppose I should have dared the experiment of wearing them as I have done, for a whole year now, at every large assemblage I have attended?"

"Millicent! Millicent, is this true?" He looked more than angry, more than dismayed. She herself seemed astonished at the intensity of the emotions she had aroused.

"Yes," she returned, "it is true." And her glance took in the face of her son standing abashed and troubled beside his bride. "This I was doing for you," she declared. "While you were seeking inspiration and delight from the smile of Philippa Irwin, I was meeting the eyes of the world with a circle of false gems about my throat, and in my heart the dread of such a scene as this, with its worse to-morrow."

"Mother—"

"No words now. I have done with you, Lawrence Sutton; let me see if I am to lose a husband as well as a son."

But Mr. Winchester was in no mood for sentiment. He had flung the glittering bauble from him, and was standing with clenched hands and working brow near the threshold of the door. As she spoke he flung the door open, and when she ceased he gave her one look, and passing out into the hall, disappeared from view.

She stood still and made no effort to follow him.

"It is the deception," I heard her murmur. "He could not

care for a few thousands so much as this." And then her haughty lip trembled, her imperious air gave way, and tottering toward the door, she held her two hands out in seeming forgetfulness of everything but her love for her husband. "William!" she cried, "William!"

But her son was already between her and the door.

"Mother!" he exclaimed, "you shall hear me. Indifferent as you consider me to have been, this debt I have owed you has weighed heavily upon me. Of course I knew nothing of the sacrifice you had made in giving me the large sum you did. I supposed it came, as you led me to suppose, from your husband; but, even so, it has troubled me and caused me many an anxious thought as to how I was to repay you. I did not find a way. But to prove to you that my remorse did not expend itself entirely in thought, I will now reveal to you the secret of my absence night after night. I am working, mother, working like a slave, for a position which, if once obtained, will give me support for my wife, and a pretty sum over every year for my mother. There is a likelihood that I shall get it, and if, in that event, I allow myself one luxury or Philippa one gewgaw till those you parted with for my sake are paid for, then say you are done with Lawrence Sutton, but not now, not while there is any hope of his proving himself your son, indeed."

But the barrier he had raised between them by his marriage was too formidable to be overthrown in an instant; and with some parting words of scorn she left him, and I heard her go up to her own room.

I hoped they would follow her, and so allow me to escape, but they had too much to say to each other, too many explanations to make. I had to be present at another confidential interview. Philippa, who, the moment they were left alone, had assumed a totally different bearing from that which seemed natural to her in Mrs. Winchester's presence, waited for her husband's first emotion of grief to subside, then turned to him, and taking his two hands in hers, drew him down beside her on the sofa.

"Lawrence," said she, with a womanly sweetness inexpressibly winning after the scene of stormy passions which had just passed, "do you think you can ever forgive me?"

"Forgive you, my heart's idol! What have I to forgive you for? The consolation that you give me for my past, the hope that you bring me for my future?"

"No, no," she murmured; "for having married you; for having—"

"Philippa!" he cried, lifting her face with the tenderest touch, and gazing long and earnestly into her eyes, "you are my wife. The holy words that made us one have hardly ceased to echo. Do not let us mar the moment, which can never come again, by any expression of doubt as regards the wisdom or the happiness of what we have done. Let us enjoy the delight of being all in all to each other, leaving to future hours, perhaps, the grief of knowing that, in seeking our own welfare, we have had to inflict disappointment upon others."

"But—but—" she faltered, "you do not understand. I allude to my marrying you to-night, in this haste, contrary to all my declarations and every resolution I had formed."

"And do you think I blame you for that? That my heart gave anything but a leap of joy when you stopped me in the hall and whispered in my ear, 'I am ready, Lawrence, ready to do what you so often have urged me to do. I will marry you to-night if you say so'?"

"Oh!" she cried, and a flush of shame crept over her face, growing lovelier with every moment that passed till I wondered I had not seen at first glance that she was beautiful; "you reproach me with every word; you make me feel that there is no one less deserving of such faith and devotion than Philippa Irwin."

"Philippa Sutton, darling; there is a difference," he smiled.

The words seemed to strike her. She looked at him very earnestly for a moment.

"Yes," she assented. "What were wisdom in Philippa Irwin may not be wisdom in Philippa Sutton. But truth is always wisdom, and I cannot enter upon our married life with the shadow of a falsehood on my heart. At the risk of losing your love, of seeing you turn away from me never to come back, I must be frank with you and open to the very heart's core. Lawrence, I would not have married you to-night if—if it had not been for the disappearance of those diamonds."

"Philippa!"

"I know, I know I should have trusted you. That I should have seen and felt that you were incapable of doing so mean and wicked a thing as—as my suspicions suggested to me, but, coming up-stairs while your mother was below, I had seen you pass into her room on tiptoe, stay but a moment, and then come creeping out again, thrusting something that glittered into your breast. I had seen this; and though I thought nothing of it at the moment I—I did fear and tremble when from the back room, into which I had stepped, I beheld her come back, walk over to the mantel-piece where she stood for a moment gazing at her jewel-case, and then, rushing to the window and throwing it open, run out again into the hall crying that her diamonds were gone and that a thief must have crawled in from the street and taken them while she was below. For—it is my only excuse, Lawrence—I could not dream she had taken advantage of that moment's pause before the mantel to snatch the jewels from their case and hide them in her own bosom. That would imply a knowledge of facts and motives to which I was necessarily a stranger. I could only think she was influenced in her action by a conviction that one she loved had done this act, and this apparent conviction of hers awakened mine; for she was a woman and a mother, and knew, as I believed, her own son well, while I was but a simple girl who loved. Yet see, yet see, she was the one who did the wrong, if wrong were done, while you—" Philippa's head sank on her breast and the tears came.

He let her weep for a moment; then with a slow and mechanical motion he thrust his hand into his breast and took out a simple bracelet made of silver coils and held it towards her.

"This is what I went for," said he, "and this is what I brought out. I had seen it lying on the sofa, Philippa, when I went in before dinner, and my heart coveted it and my lips burned to kiss it, and—"

"O Lawrence!" was her cry, "my bracelet!" and then there was silence, during which he sat with his eyes on her face in a mute reproach, evidently worse to her than death. At last she could bear it no longer, and lifting her head she gave him one look.

It seemed to recall him to himself. Grasping her hand, he uttered one short sentence, but that was full of meaning. It was this: "And yet you married me!"

The pallor of her cheek disappeared in a flush that made her absolutely dazzling.

"I loved you," she murmured, "and I knew, that is, I had heard, that a wife could not be called upon to testify against her husband."

He gave a sudden cry, and his arms closed passionately round her. He did not tell her that that was an old and antiquated law, no longer in force at this day; he only whispered words of love and consolation, and when, ten minutes from that time, they left the room and I at last succeeded in escaping from my hiding-place and from the house, it was with the conviction that I had left two noble hearts behind me, whose happiness, if not their worldly prosperity, was assured.

Early the next morning I sent a line to Mr. Randall effectually relieving him from all the doubts I had left in his mind as to Mr. Sutton's integrity and genuine change of character. This duty done I thought the story ended, as far as outsiders were concerned. But it was not so. Scarcely three days had elapsed when New York society was startled and her business men confounded by the announcement that Mr. Winchester had disappeared from town, leaving debts of an enormous nature behind him and no assets wherewith to pay those debts. Then and not till then did I understand his passionate anxiety about the diamonds. To a man on the verge of ruin twenty-five thousand dollars may hold out the promise of salvation. At all events it is a convenient sum with which to facilitate flight, and its loss must have been a heavy blow to him.

His wife, whose pride was perhaps phenomenal in its way, never recovered from the shock thus given her. When the last load was driven away from the house she was obliged to abandon, her indomitable spirit broke, and it was a depressed and humiliated woman that at last consented to take up her abode with the son she had cast off and the woman she once looked upon with contempt.

ONE HOUR MORE.

I was walking along the Rue des Martins. I was thoughtful, for I had just been witness to a sight that greatly moved me. My duties as a reporter for one of the large Paris dailies had taken me to Havre just as the ship came in which brought the Communists home from exile, and, hardened as I confess myself to be to the more frequent aspects of human suffering, the sight of those men crowding forward to catch the first glimpse of the friends who had come to meet them, touched me with a feeling that was not unlike compassion. I was thinking of them and wondering what sort of fate awaited the older men I saw there, when a sudden cry from over my head startled me from my musings, and looking up, I saw a woman peering out of the top window of a wretched apartment.

She showed such signs of distress in her countenance that I at once knew something terrible had occurred within, and foreseeing matter for my next article, I immediately entered the house.

I found myself confronted by frightened faces everywhere. All the inmates knew that something was wrong on the top floor, but no one knew just what. They followed me when they saw me determined to find out. The consequence was that a small crowd pressed behind me as

I mounted the last stair; a crowd that seemed to awe if not alarm the trembling woman who awaited me at the top, for she started back as she saw it, muttering to herself:

"Mon Dieu! Elise never had so many visitors before!"

A door swinging on its hinges at the right of this woman at once attracted my attention. Advancing with small ceremony, I threw it open. I found my expectations more than realized. On the bed before me lay the outstretched form of a woman, the pallor and fixedness of whose face bespoke death. Not a natural death either, for she was dressed as if she had just come in from the street, with the exception of her bonnet, which lay on the floor beside her, where it had evidently been flung by a careless hand. Otherwise the room was in perfect order, I may even say in holiday order. From the work neatly folded on the shelf to the small bunch of fresh flowers that adorned a table set out with an untouched meal—a meal which even in the hurried glance I gave it I saw was arranged for two—all bespoke one of those rare days of rest and relaxation which now and then enter a French working-woman's life.

But the dead face on the pillow—what did it betoken? Had murder crept into this humble dwelling or was it a suicide I beheld? Involuntarily drawing nearer the bed, I looked at the face before me more closely. It was that of a young and pretty woman, and while touchingly meagre and sad was touchingly delicate also. It was almost a lady's face, and had it not been for the evidence of toil displayed by the hands I should certainly have taken it for such. As it was I could not doubt that a real working-woman lay there, though from the marks of refinement observable in her dress and the presence of certain choice books on the shelf over her head, she was evidently a woman of taste and education.

"It is a suicide!" I declared, seeing a bottle of well-known poison protruding from under the pillow.

"Of course it is," murmured a voice over my shoulder. "Don't you see what she has written on that paper near you?"

I glanced down at the table by which I was standing and saw a sheet of common note paper, inscribed with these words:

"My husband was a Communist and was exiled. He was all I had in the world, and since his departure I have only lived to see him again. But I have had no news, no letter. I have been patient, however, for I have waited for this day. But it has come, and it has not brought him. I went to the ship myself and looked at every man who left it. He was not amongst them. So now I know he is dead. That being so, there is no more reason why I should live.

"Elise Picard."

Involuntarily I had read these words aloud. A murmur of almost ferocious sympathy greeted them from the crowd that had gathered at my back. The sound disturbed me, for my thoughts had flown at once to the ship and that throng of pale and eager men I had myself seen in the morning. I felt a strange inclination to be alone, and shouldering my way out past the humble table set so touchingly with a meal never destined to be eaten, I made my way into the hall.

But before I could reach the stairs a woman advanced and laid her hand on my arm. It was the same who had given the first alarm.

"Would you mind stepping into my room a minute?" she asked. "There is something I would like to show you."

Naturally curious, I followed at once.

"What is it?" I inquired, when we were shut in an apartment of even scantier proportions than the one we had just left.

"Only some letters which Elise put into my hands a little while ago—before—before she showed herself so tired of life. You see we had been neighbors here, and Elise, though she was far above me—she was born a lady, Monsieur—was kind to me, and told me many of her griefs. I could not appreciate them all, for I never was educated; but I do know what it is to love, for I had a good husband myself once, and so when she spoke of him I could understand. And there was not a day she did not speak of him. It was as if he always stood at her side. Her very eyes had a far-away look, as if she was seeing something more than the rest of us did. I used to have an awe of her, especially when she smiled to herself."

"It is very sad," said I. "And did she never hear from him after he was taken away?"

"No. She never doubted that he lived, though, and would come back. 'I feel it here,' she used to say, laying her hand on her heart. 'Why else do I live?' she would add. Only yesterday her face was like the sunlight. 'I am sure he will come home with the rest,' she cried, 'and then I shall know why he did not write.' Did you see how she had his dinner ready? I went with her to market, and it was touching to hear her say, 'I must get this,' or 'I must get that; he used to like it so well.'"

"Did you go with her to the wharf?" I asked, willing to learn all I could.

"No, Monsieur. She didn't seem to want me to. But I shall never forget the look she gave me as she went out of the door. There wasn't any doubt in it. To my foolish mind it seemed to say, 'I shall never be lonely in this room any more.' Mon Dieu! when I think how that look must have brightened when she saw the poor wanderers crowding forward out of the ship, and then have faded away to what it was when she came back alone, my heart is ready to break.”

“You saw her, then, after her return?”

“A moment. She came to my door with the letters you have there. As soon as I saw her I knew what had happened, but I couldn’t speak. My tongue seemed to cleave to the roof of my mouth. You see, I had been as sure as she that he would be there with the rest.”

“Didn’t you say anything then?”

“Not a word; she didn’t give me a chance. ‘My husband is dead,’ was her greeting as she opened the door. ‘I looked in the face of every one of the exiles as they left the ship, and he was not there. I want to leave these letters with you; they were meant for him.’ And without looking me in the face she laid the package down with a slow stiff movement, as if she were already half dead herself, then went out and closed the door. There was something in her look which told me not to follow her.”

“But weren’t you afraid of what she would do? Didn’t you fear she might commit suicide?”

“No, sir. Yet if I had I don’t think I should have followed her.” Then as I looked up surprised the good woman hastened to say:

“It is a sadder story than you think. If you care to hear—”

I did not wait for her to finish.

“Tell me all you know about her,” said I.

The woman eagerly complied. The facts which she gave me, together with a few others afterwards gleaned by me from a different source, form the basis of the following history, a history which I am sure you will pardon me for giving in my own words rather than in those of my informants:

Elise Lepage was not a beauty, yet in her earlier youth,

at least, she possessed a charm which always insured her the admiration and very often the love of those with whom she came in contact. Her father, who was a musician of somewhat mediocre talent, recognized this charm, and in his simple way calculated upon its winning her a suitable husband, notwithstanding his small means and her consequent lack of a dowry. To him she was a paragon, and when, at the close of a long day of unremitting labor at the piano, he saw her approaching him in a dainty fresh robe ready for their usual walk on the boulevard, his face would light up with such pride and joy that the loving girl who watched him felt the tear gush to her eye at the same moment the smile rose to her lip.

They lived in a plain but sufficiently comfortable apartment, and had for neighbors two young men by the name of Picard,—brothers. These two young men occupied the apartment above them; and one of them, the youngest, having some taste for music, a natural acquaintance had sprung up between him and M. Lepage, which presently involved the older brother and Mlle. Lepage. The consequence was that Jean, the elder brother, fell in love with the fresh, charming young girl, and, being himself a man of no conventional prejudices—the future Communist in fact— he offered to marry her without any other fortune than that of her youth and many virtues. The old father was delighted. First, because he felt himself failing in health and was anxious to see his darling's future secured; and secondly, because he liked this man better than any one else in the world save and excepting always his dear and much admired daughter. Why he felt this extraordinary affection for a man of whom he was forced to acknowledge to himself he knew but little, he could not have told had he tried. Certainly it was not because he understood him, for he did not; neither was it because the other possessed attractions of a peculiar or marked nature. Jean Picard was not handsome, nor was he even gifted in manner or conversation, yet old Mr. Lepage loved him and hailed the prospect of his being his son-in-law with as much fervor as if he were the owner of millions instead of being the physician of one of the poorest and worst paying quarters in the whole city. He trusted him, and that fact, perhaps, illustrates the character of the two men. For Jean Picard was to be trusted in all matters of the heart and conscience; it was only his head that was at fault, or, perhaps, I should say his temperament. He had inherited traditions of the First Revolution, and believed absolutely in the might of the people. But of this he had nothing to say in those days, his head and his heart being joined in the one wish, the one hope, the one purpose, to make Elise his wife.

The evening which he had chosen to speak to M. Lepage—he had never breathed a word of his desires to Elise herself—was, as he afterwards remembered, an especially beautiful one. The moon was shining, and as, filled with the joy of a successful suit, he stepped from the apartment of M. Lepage, something in the quiet beauty of this round and serene orb touched the poetry that exists with all true love in the heart, and drew him, in spite of his usually active ways, to a window opening from the corridor on to a small garden belonging to the concierge. He was looking from this window and dreaming of Elise, when his glance, which had been mechanically fixed upon a leafy retreat beneath him, became earnest, deep, and inquiring, and with a startled gesture of surprise, he bent forward and listened as if his life depended upon his hearing what went on in the garden below him. Had he seen anything which threatened his happiness, and if so, what?

His firm and controlled countenance tells little, but his wandering look and the unsteady step with which he leaves the window and betakes himself to his own room bespeak strong agitation. If we follow him and watch him as a half hour later he slowly rouses from the deep and troubled brooding into which he had sunk immediately upon his entrance, and turning towards the door, waits with a look not to be mistaken for the advance of the step just becoming audible upon the stairs, we shall undoubtedly learn from his own lips what it is that has disturbed him so deeply at a moment he esteemed himself so profoundly blessed.

Yet is he going to speak? His lips have opened, his face has assumed a terrible expression, he has even advanced two paces toward the door to meet the expected comer, when suddenly he pauses. The face he sees before him is not the one he anticipated. It is that of his brother, to be sure, but it does not wear the look he had schooled himself to meet, the triumphant look that goes with happy love, however wrongfully it may be won. The surprise upsets him, and for a moment the words falter on his tongue, then all his manhood re-asserts itself, and imperiously beckoning his brother to enter, he closes the door and stands with the handle still in his grasp, looking at Camille.

"You are in trouble," said he shortly. "What is it?" Then as he saw his brother start and uneasily drop his eyes, added bitterly: "Have you told her what you are, and does she refuse to marry you?"

Camille, who was of a fiery nature, but who for certain reasons stood somewhat in awe of his brother, looked for a moment as if he could have leaped at his throat; but he restrained himself, and while the veins swelled on his forehead and his face grew fiery red, he stammered:

"Whom do you mean by her? I do not understand you."

"That is not true; you understand me perfectly," was the rude but brave Jean's straightforward response. "But if you must have names I allude to Elise, the pure, innocent, high-minded girl whom by arts I do not profess to understand you have succeeded in pleasing, till, for aught I know, she considers you a model of virtue and goodness."

"And if she did?" broke in the other impetuously.

Jean drew a deep breath and stepped slowly back.

"I should undeceive her," he declared, "if by the act I alienated her good-will forever."

Camille, who for some cause did not resent the first clause of this sentence, started at the second, and gave his brother a sharp look.

"Mon Dieu!" exclaimed he, with as much wonder as jealousy in his tone. "Do you love her too?"

The look which Jean turned upon his brother made that other's weak and selfish heart stand still.

"I love her," said he, "I will not say too, for you do not love her. Had you loved her you would have fled from her instead of using all your arts secretly to win her. A criminal—"

"Hush!" exclaimed the other, with a terrified look around him that for some reason made Jean quail with a sense of apprehension. "Do you want to draw the police upon me?"

With a stride Jean advanced upon his brother, and, laying his strong hand on his shoulders, uncompromisingly turned him towards the light.

"You tremble," he muttered under his breath. "You shrink, and your face is like marble. Mon Dieu! Camille, is there anything new?"

With a suppressed cry Camille tore himself from his brother's hands.

"Who has given you the right to question me?" he cried. "I will not have it. I have had enough of your spying." And flinging himself violently towards the door of his own room, he was on the point of disappearing from Jean's presence, when the latter, with another movement of his strong arm, drew him back and himself entered the apartment.

In an instant he came back. His face was like stone, and he had in his hand a valise fully packed, which he set heavily down on the table before Camille's eyes.

"What does this mean?" he asked. "Where are you going and why have you kept your departure a secret from me?"

For a moment the stricken Camille did not reply; then he broke down, and flinging himself on his knees, burst forth with the cry:

"I am a ruined man, Jean; I—I tried it again, and this time it will be found out. To-morrow, to-night, possibly, my employer will look over his books, and—"

"How much is it?" broke in Jean, in a low, strained voice.

"Ten thousand francs," murmured the other. "All gone."

"Lost at play?"

Camille nodded his head.

Jean drew back, covering his face for a moment with his hands.

"I have just that amount," he said, "saved up. Your employer shall have it to-morrow. As for you," he added bitterly, "I wash my hands of you. This is twice."

His voice broke, and he hurriedly withdrew to the window, as if the sight of his brother's face maddened him.

He returned almost instantly, however, and walking straight up to Camille, demanded:

"What were you doing there?" pointing sternly below. "This bag shows you intended to abscond to-night. Were you bidding her farewell or—"

He had not strength to finish, but his look filled up the hiatus left in his speech.

Camille faltered beneath that glance. If he could have seen a way to escape, his furtive, worried look showed he would have availed himself of it. But his brother's eye held him and would have the truth. With a gasp he broke forth:

"I have bidden her farewell. She does not know why I go. She loves me and she trusts me. I—I would have persuaded her to go with me if I could. I love her, I say, whatever you may call it. I love her, do you hear, and if I could have induced her to leave her father you would not have caught me in this box. It was my despair."

He stopped. There was something in Jean's face which told him that silence was better than speech at this moment. The first words of Jean convinced him of it.

"You are a villain," said he, "and the punishment of your villainy shall be a confession. I hope to marry Elise Lepage," he went on, raising his hand for silence as he saw his brother about to protest, "and I do not intend she shall waste her life in useless regrets over the loss of one so unworthy as yourself. Come, then, and in her presence, if not in that of her father, proclaim yourself the criminal that you are or—"

"Or what?" asked the other, with a wild gleam, half of defiance, half of fear.

"Or I keep my ten thousand francs and leave you to the tender mercies of a man whose justice, you have reason to know, is stronger than his mercy."

A cold sweat broke out on Camille's face. He looked at his brother with great staring eyes as if he could hardly believe in the alternative that was offered him. Seeing it, Jean continued:

"It is three years since the day I first awoke to the knowledge that I had for my brother a man who had provoked the justice of the law, and only escaped by the ignorance or blindness of those he had defrauded. In those three years I have spared nothing, either in the way of money or effort, to give you what you wanted and save you, if possible, from the repetition of your dastardly crime. How have you repaid me? By stealing the fancy of the woman I loved, or," as Camille faintly objected, "the fancy of a girl whom you knew I respected, and whom you also knew would never have given you her regard had she known your real character or suspected the shadow that hung above you. She thinks you true, you say, and trusts you. That means she will remember you lovingly in your absence, possibly wait for your return, when return you never will. Elise is too fine a girl to be thus sacrificed," asserted Jean, "and if I did not love her I should still say, 'Come below, and show yourself to her for what you are.' Better she should suffer this one shock, that in itself carries healing, than linger on for years a prey to a pain of longing that will be none the less keen because it will be so bravely hidden."

But Camille had sunk before this prospect.

"I cannot," he murmured, "I would rather go to the galleys."

Meantime, in her own little room below, Elise was bitterly weeping. She had loved Camille almost unconsciously. Not till she saw him about to leave her did she realize how deeply he had entered into her dreams and hopes. Then the mystery of his departure heightened its effect. Though the ready tale he told of the fine position which had been offered him in a mercantile house in Peru was plausible enough, there was something in his manner and the fact that he wished to carry her away with him secretly that struck an icy doubt to her heart, and, devoted as she was to him, she felt as if she would give all the world, were it hers, to throw herself into her father's arms and ask him for his sympathy and counsel. But that was expressly forbidden. Her father must know nothing of her sorrow or her love; her wilful lover would not have it. And young as she was, innocent as her thoughts were of wrong or deception, there was something in this ban laid between her and the father she so idolized, that awakened strange doubts and fears in her otherwise trusting bosom.

Her room adjoined that of M. Lepage, and more than once during her grief and tears she had heard his restless foot approach the door of communication, as though he were about to call her to him. But he did not; she was so quiet he evidently thought she was asleep, and finally all became as still in his room as it was deathlike in hers. And Elise wept on.

Suddenly there came a tap, not on the door she had been so fearful of seeing open, but on the one which led into the hall. Astonished, frightened almost, she crept to it and faintly asked who was there. A woman's voice answered. It was the concierge, who handed her a small note. Hurriedly lighting her candle, Elise unfolded it and read:

"Mademoiselle—It is indispensable that I should have a few minutes' conversation with you to-night. It is 10 o'clock, therefore your father has retired and your little sitting-room will be free. I shall not come alone.

"Respectfully,   Jean Picard."

A whirl of thoughts swept through Elise's brain. She felt dizzy, almost sick, but she did not hesitate. Opening the door into her father's room, she glided in. All was quiet. The good man was evidently asleep. Hastily crossing the floor, she gained the little sitting-room beyond, and, closing the door behind her, struck a light. Then, stopping but a moment to regain breath and still the nervous beatings of her heart, she approached the hall door and softly opened it. A low cry escaped her as she did so, the two men standing on the threshold bore in their countenances such signs of subdued agitation.

"What is it?" she faintly breathed, falling back with a slow step as they entered. "Why are you here so late? And together?" she could not help adding, as her eyes roamed from the one face to the other, both so white, both so drawn, both so filled with that strange look which a woman only sees on the countenance of the man who loves her.

As Camille did not answer, Jean replied:

"Mademoiselle," said he, "I have come here on a very disagreeable duty. I have come to hear my brother tell you the truth. Camille, speak."

Camille, thus abjured, cast one glance of burning anguish at his brother, then in a voice so unnatural Elise could scarcely believe it his own, exclaimed bitterly:

"He wishes me to tell you I am a villain. It is not a pleasant thing to say of one's self, Mademoiselle, but it is true. I am a villain, and—and I advise you to forget me."

The deep misery expressed in his tones shook Jean a little, but he was inexorable. Giving one glance at Elise, who, seemingly turned into stone by the terrible nature of her lover's words, stood breathless and pale before them, he said:

"It is not enough, Camille; tell her why you go away to-night. Tell her it is a flight."

"You have said it," murmured the other, half savagely; then as Jean remained unchanged in look and attitude, cried harshly: "Mademoiselle, I am unworthy of your attention. I—I am no longer an honest man. I—have—"

"Stolen," added a deep, firm voice.

The silence that followed this word was such as could be felt.

"And you wished to take me with you!" were the words that first interrupted it.

"I love you," murmured Camille in a broken, miserable tone.

Elise turned slowly away.

"My father! my father!" burst involuntarily from her lips, and she held out her arms in dumb entreaty to the door that separated her from her beloved parent.

Instantly and as if in answer to her appeal, a strange murmur arose from that room, an inarticulate, almost an agonized murmur that struck terror to the hearts of those who heard it.

"My father!" again cried Elise, and this time she rushed at the door and tore it widely open. Her father lay stretched before her on the floor, having evidently fallen in his efforts to answer her summons.

It was midnight, two hours after the fatal event recorded in the above lines. Around the bedside of M. Lepage were grouped a physician, a priest, the concierge, Jean Picard, and his daughter. Camille was already far away.

The physician had given them no hope. In an hour or less the poor musician's soul would be far away. He was sensible of it himself. Upon his first return to consciousness he had said:

"This is death."

Elise, overwhelmed as she was, could not weep. Her one thought seemed to be: "Supposing I had listened to Camille's entreaties, and had been flying from Paris in this terrible hour!"

Jean Picard, on the contrary, shed more than one tear. Perhaps the restraint he had put upon himself in the tragic scene which had preceded this catastrophe was having its revenge upon him now, or perhaps the look of peace with which the old man surveyed him and his daughter, standing, as they were, side by side, struck him by its contrast to the sad reality. It was midnight, as I have said, and the clock was striking. As it ceased, the dying man spoke:

"May I not see your two hands joined?" he asked, gazing tenderly at Jean and Elise.

As though a thunderbolt had fallen at her feet, Elise started and fell back. Jean hastily cleared the room and then leading her gently up to the bedside, he said solemnly:

"Mademoiselle, you must pardon your father. Three hours ago I had the honor to ask of him your hand in marriage, and he had the goodness to accord it to me. He does not know that we have had no conversation on this matter since, and that therefore such words must fall upon you with a shock."

"Did you—were you—" she stammered, "thinking of this when you—"

"Mademoiselle," interrupted Jean, "whatever I have ever done or said has been more for your sake than my own; believe that." And he threw a glance at M. Lepage which she could not fail to understand.

Hiding her face in her hands, Elise knelt by the bedside.

She could feel her father's hand fall on her head, caressingly, lingeringly. In a minute more she heard him say:

"He is a good man; you will marry him, Elise?" Then as she did not answer, he added softly, "I should die so happy."

With a spring she stood upright. "Jean Picard," she said, "do you wish me for your wife?"

A great light which she could not help noticing in that solemn hour settled slowly over all his face.

"There is nothing I wish so much," he answered; "it has been my dream for months."

"After what you know of my heart?" she murmured, but so low the dying man could not hear her.

"Elise," was the equally low answer, "I do not expect you to love me just yet, but you need a protector; let me be that protector. You need some one to comfort you and provide you with a home; let me be that friend, and I will trust my love to make you satisfied in the end."

"You are a good man," she murmured, in unconscious repetition of her father's words; and, scarcely knowing what she did, she laid her hand in his, seeing more clearly the smile that parted her poor father's lips at the action than the solemn look above with which Jean Picard accepted the trust thus imparted to him.

And so it was that Elise Lepage became the wife of Jean Picard, and a tragedy of the heart was begun which ended, as we have seen, in her death. For Elise was a conscientious woman, and once married set all her hopes on the prospect of some day becoming as much a wife in heart as she was now in name. But that heart was at first too sore with the violent wrench it had sustained to experience much beyond gratitude, and months rolled by without Jean Picard discovering in his young wife's studiously kind manner any token of that passion which informed his own life. Yet the germ if not the flower of it was in her breast. Unconsciously to herself her husband was becoming all in all to her, but the feeling she experienced for him was so different from that she had given to his unworthy brother that she did not recognize it for what it was, and called it simply friendship.

The stirring events of the war and the opening days of the Commune did not alter matters. A numbness seemed to settle upon Elise as she saw her husband gradually identifying himself with a cause she both mistrusted and feared. That her coldness drove him into the savage warfare of the barricades she did not think. She knew him well enough to perceive that, however it was with others, with him it was a matter of conscience to uphold what he called the rights of the people. And perceiving this, she did not lose her respect for him, though her terrors accumulated and an element of dread came into her regard for him which caused her less and less to suspect the true nature of the emotions he inspired.

Nor did the culmination of his career and his subsequent downfall fully awaken her. Like a dream the dreadful days passed in which he was tried, condemned, and sentenced to exile; like a dream came the time of parting. And not till she felt herself torn from his clasping arms did she realize that life was ending for her, that the moment of death had come and she had never told him she loved him. Making a vigorous effort, for her senses seemed to be leaving her, she turned, all tremulous with passionate feeling, and holding out her arms to him, was about to utter what would have illumined his exile, when doubt, that black shadow of the soul, glided again across her spirit, and, saying to herself, "'Tis but a boundless regret at the loss of his goodness," she permitted herself only to cry:

"Good-by, Jean. I will be true to you in your absence, and work if need be with my own hands, to sustain myself till you come back."

His sad smile told her, when too late, what she had done, or rather had omitted to do.

The memory of that smile never left her. It haunted her day and night. The struggle into which she was forced for her daily bread only served to perpetuate her remorse. From a somewhat practical woman she became a dreamer of dreams. All her soul centred in the one wish, the one hope of seeing him again, if only to whisper in his ear the truth that was every day becoming more and more apparent in her own heart. She dared not write it to him. The first few dutiful letters she had sent had never been answered, and she was of a temperament that made it impossible for her to risk the chance of her heart's story falling into alien or unsympathetic hands. But she could not entirely smother her desire for utterance. So the letters came to be written, which, though never sent, contained the beatings of her heart through that long and dreary separation, letters which she evidently fully expected would meet his eyes, and tell him in sweetest language what her own tongue had failed to do on that memorable day of their parting.

But hope cherished to the last, went suddenly out like a candle extinguished. The ship which was to bring the exiles home arrived in safety, and she saw it and saw them, but did not see him. The blow was fatal. Without asking a question, or doubting the doom which had fallen upon him and therefore upon her, she returned home and put, as we have seen, a desperate end to her own life. Love long repressed had had its full revenge. She could not live without its object.

Such was the story of Elise Picard, told me in substance by the good woman who had befriended her and in detail by the letters she had left behind her in this same woman's charge. I had scarcely reached the end, that is, had scarcely laid the last letter down, when a sudden hubbub rose in the hall without, followed by a pitiful low moan which somehow or other awoke in me a peculiar apprehension. Springing to the door I flung it open. Never shall I forget the picture that met my eyes. Frozen each in his place by some great emotion, the eager crowd before me stood silent, aghast, gazing at a figure that, emaciated almost beyond the semblance of a man, crouched against the wall which led towards the room of death.

The hush, the intolerable anguish expressed by that form, bent almost double by the sudden weight of woe which had fallen upon it, touched me to the quick. Grasping the hand of the first person I could reach, I asked:

"Who is he? What does this mean?"

But I did not need an answer to my question; I knew without words that Jean Picard stood before me.

I learned afterwards that he was among the men that passed before her eyes on the wharf, but he was so changed by disease and grief she had not recognized him. He had been spending the last two hours in a search for her.